50 Life a
from Steve Jobs

Written by: George Ilian

Cover Illustration: Iren Flowers

Copyright © 2015

All Rights Reserved

Warning-Disclaimer

More Books By George Ilian

George Ilian is the author of many inspirational books and guides how to make money online.

His mission is to help you have all the money and freedom you need to go and live anywhere you want and travel around the world. It is all possible with the money that you can make online, giving you the ability to have everything you've ever wanted—and more!

Welcome

Geniuses come in every shape and colour, and when they step into a room, we almost expect them to glow, or buzz with a special energy that sets them apart from the rest of us. To many people, the slightly-built, greying and bespectacled gentlemen in a long-sleeved black turtleneck and blue Levi jeans would never have warranted a second look. Steve Jobs was extraordinary in his apparent ordinariness.

When you peel back the layers, however, Steve Jobs was far from ordinary. His far-sightedness, persistence and absolute faith in the Apple brand and Apple products catapult-ed the company from nowhere in 1976, to global superstar status today: Apple is the second largest (but best-known) consumer information technology company in the world; it's the world's largest publicly traded corpora-tion; Apple's world-wide revenue in 2014 to-talled $182 billion; and at the end of 2014, Apple became the first American company ever to be valued at more than $700 billion. If you want to understand Apple, you need to think big. If you, like Jobs, want to conceive a success story like Apple in the first place, you need to have the unrestricted imagination and ambition to think even bigger than that.

The birth and re-birth of Apple were by no means his only achievements, however: Jobs also founded the pioneering NeXT, which would prove to be his segue back to Apple in 1997. He bought Pixar from Lucasfilm and made it a blockbuster success, delivering the likes of *Toy Story, Finding Nemo* and *Monsters, Inc.* to delight a generation of children (and their parents) around the world. And when he sold Pixar to Disney, he became Disney's largest shareholder and a valuable member of the board.

Collectively through his achievements, Jobs would transform the world of consumer technology, not only in computing but in music and digital animation too. He would bring lines of previously inconceivable products to the market place, sell those products direct to consumers, and make computing cooler than it had ever been before. He has quite rightly been acclaimed as the entrepreneur, and the CEO, of his generation, and one of the greatest innovators of all time.

In this book you will find an introduction to Steve Jobs, his life and work. It is by no means encyclopaedic, but it is not intended to be. The narrative is told chronology and in bite-size chunks so that you can dip in and learn about a specific period in his life, a particular project or achievement. For ease of learning, and to make you think about what Jobs can teach you in your own life and business, there are 50 short lessons, one at the end of each section, that sums up the most important points to remember. We cannot all become Steve Jobs or found a company as game changing Apple, but we can make the most of his example and become ever more successful in the things that we do.

Part 1: A Genius Was Born

Steve Jobs was born in San Francisco on February 24, 1955. His biological parents, Syrian-born Abdulfatah "John" Jandali, a graduate student at the University of Wisconsin, and his mother, a Swiss-American undergraduate named Joanne Carole Schieble, weren't planning on parenthood so soon, and even after Schieble fell pregnant with Jobs, her conservative father refused to let them marry. They gave Jobs up for adoption as soon as he was born, and he was adopted by Paul and Clara Jobs, who had been married since 1946 but were sadly unable to have their own children. Schieble had specified that the baby should only be adopted by college graduates, but although the Jobs both had relatively little formal education, a compromise was struck when they promised to encourage, and financially support, the child through college.

Lesson No. 1: Your start in life is not what is most important: it is where you end up that counts.

Although many adopted children describe feelings of loss, abandonment or somehow not belonging, Jobs had no such concerns: he believed he was not abandoned but rather chosen, stated that Paul and Clara Jobs "were my parents 1,000%," and in his authorised biography reiterated, "Paul and Clara are 100% my parents. And Joanna and Abdulfatah—are only a sperm and an egg bank. It's not rude, it is the truth." The Jobs lavished affection on their adopted son and provided him with a comfortable, stable childhood.

Lesson No. 2: Don't be afraid to speak the truth.

The Jobs family moved to Mountain View, which would later become the heart of Silicon Valley, when Jobs was five, and shortly after the move, they adopted a daughter, Patty. The Jobs family was complete, and Jobs' childhood was stable and unremarkable. His mother worked as an accountant for Varian Associates, one of California's first high-tech firms, and his father worked as a mechanic and carpenter.

Young Jobs was encouraged to work alongside his father in the workshop, and as a result he picked up many practical skills. Jobs learned how things work, and how to make them with his own hands. The Jobs were unpretentious, practical people, and their work ethic was passed on to both of their children.

Lesson No. 3: Practical skills and hard work underpin achievement.

Jobs was a smart child, scoring elementary school test scores two grades higher than his age, but he didn't apply himself particularly and he was often disruptive in class. He skipped a year of school, and whilst at Homestead High School in Cupertino forged a close friendship with Bill Fernandez (who later became Apple Computers' first employee), who introduced Jobs to his neighbour, Steve Wozniak. Together, Jobs and Wozniak would transform the world of technology.

Lesson No. 4: Personal relationships are vital to success.

Jobs graduated from high school in 1972 and, true to his parents' promise, they enrolled him at Reed College in Portland, Oregon, despite the fact that they could ill afford to do so. Jobs lasted just six months at Reed before dropping out. He slept on friends' dorm room floors, recycled Coca Cola bottles to earn a few cents, and ate free meals at a Hare Krishna temple. This could well have been the end of Jobs' story, but just because he had no interest in conventional education didn't mean he'd be a life-long underachiever.

Lesson No. 5: Nothing is beneath you when you're starting out.

The same year, Wozniak designed and built a new version the iconic arcade game *Pong* and he asked his friend Jobs to present it to Atari Inc. at their head office. Thinking that Jobs was the creator, Atari offered him a job as a technician. Jobs did not dissuade them of their view.

Jobs worked for the company throughout the early 1970s, but took a seven-month sabbatical to India, where he stayed at an ashram and sought spiritual enlightenment from a variety of religious teachers. He studied Zen Buddhism seriously, considered becoming a monk at the Eihei-ji temple in Japan, and remained a practising Buddhist throughout his life.

Lesson No. 6: Know yourself.

Jobs' travels in this period had a profound effect on him. When asked about the importance of gaining experience by Wired magazine in 1996, he said:

Unfortunately, that's too rare a commodity. A lot of people in our industry haven't had very diverse experiences. So they don't have enough dots to connect, and they end up with very linear solutions without a broad perspective on the problem. The broader one's understanding of the human experience, the better design we will have.

When asked by the *New York Times* for his opinion on Bill Gates, he drew parallels with his own life and implied Gates would have done better had he followed suit:

I just think he [Gates] and Microsoft are a bit narrow. He'd be a broader guy if he had dropped acid once or gone off to an ashram when he was younger.

Jobs was adamant that his cross-cultural experience as a young man in India, and his countercultural values, were essential to the development of his thinking. He believed that unless you shared those experiences and values, you would not be able to relate to him. Right from the beginning, Jobs wanted to be seen as an outsider, a rebel, and a maverick.

Lesson No. 7: Be open to new ideas and experiences.

When Jobs returned to the US after his sabbatical, Jobs and Wozniak worked on more arcade games for Atari, and also on blue box telephone dialling devices. In both cases their focus was on reducing the numbers of chips used in the circuit board design so that they were cheaper to manufacture. The two men experimented with different technologies and sold their blue boxes illegally as they circumvented long-distance call charges for phones.

Computing as a discipline was in its earliest phase in the mid-1970s, but both Jobs and Wozniak joined the Homebrew Computer Club in Menlo Park, a group of technically minded individuals who met, experimented, chatted and traded parts as a hobby. It was at the first Homebrew meeting that Jobs saw an MITS Altair, one of the earliest microcomputers, and Wozniak subsequently recalled that it was at that moment he was inspired to design the first Apple product.

Lesson No. 8: Keep abreast of new technologies.

Part 2: The Birth of Apple

Steve Jobs might well be the famous face of Apple, but there's a strong case that Steve Wozniak was the brains of the outfit, at least in the company's earliest phase. Inspired by the electronics samples he and Jobs had seen at the Homebrew Computer Club, Wozniak built the Apple I personal computer kit, a pre-assembled circuit board. Users had to add their own monitor, power supply and keyboard, and the Apple I had just 4 KB of memory.

Lesson No. 9: The only way to do great work is to love what you do.

Even if Wozniak was the technical whizz kid, it was Jobs who was the one with a head for figures and who saw the commercial value of Wozniak's invention. Jobs obtained the first order, for 50 machines, from the Byte Store, a local computer store in Mountain View. The order was worth $25,000, and the parts alone cost $20,000, and as the components had been bought on 30-day credit, all 50 had to be built and delivered to Byte within 10 days. The Apple I went on sale in July 1976, and a single unit cost $666.66 (equivalent to $2,763 today when adjusted for inflation).

Lesson No. 10: Know your own strengths and those of the people around you.

Apple was incorporated as a company in January 1977, by which time the Apple I was selling well. The sole shareholders of the company at the time of incorporation were Jobs and Wozniak as they had bought out a third partner, Ronald Wayne, for $800. Wayne, who was older and, unlike his co-founders, had personal assets, thought the venture was too risky, though he'd come to rue his premature exit. In February 2015, Apple's value exceeded $700 billion, If Wayne had kept his 10% stock until then, it would have been worth approximately $60 billion.

Lesson No. 11: Be prepared to take a gamble.

To grow the company whilst allowing Wozniak to develop new products, Jobs had to take responsibility for raising substantial funding. He convinced Mike Markkula, an angel investor who had made his own fortune from stock options he acquired working at Intel, to provide an equity investment of $80,000 and an additional loan of $170,000. In exchange, Markkula took one-third of Apple's shares, and became employee No.3.

Markkula was a trained engineer, and he bought both experience and credibility to the new company. He wrote programs for Apple II, beta-tested products, introduced Michael Scott as Apple's first CEO and President, and helped Jobs obtain additional venture capital. Jobs was humble enough to recognise his own limitations, to watch what Markkula did attentively, and to learn from him. For Jobs, Markkula was both a business partner and a mentor, and this period in the late 1970s was probably Jobs' most important period of education in life.

Lesson No. 12: Choose your investors wisely as they can offer more than just funding.

Apple's second project, the not-so-imaginatively named Apple II, was launched in April

1977 and, unlike the Apple I, it had a commercial launch at the West Coast Computer Faire. It was streets ahead of its competitors for three reasons: Apple II had cell-based colour graphics; it was based on open architecture; and you could use a regular cassette tape for storage. Later versions could take a 5.5" floppy disk instead of a cassette tape, and there was a custom-built interface called Disk II. The Apple II was only one of three computers on the market released specifically for home users. Collectively these three computers were known as the 1977 Trinity, and the other two models were the Commodore PET and the Tandy Corporations TRS-80.

Lesson No. 13: Be innovative.

The first computer spreadsheet program, VisiCalc, was released in the middle of 1979 by Software Arts. It was one of the first pieces of truly user-friendly software, it retailed for under $100, and, most importantly of all, for the first 12 months it was available, it was only compatible with the Apple II. Users bought the Apple II specifically to run VisiCalc, and the Apple II ceased being a novelty item for tech geeks and became an essential part of the office furniture. Apple thus made the transition into the business market without having to make changes to their product or to spend a fortune on advertising.

Apple's growth accelerated throughout the late 1970s. Jobs ran a professional team that included both computer designers and those who worked on the production line, and together they looked how to utilise existing products and ideas in innovative ways. Jobs took his team to Xerox PARC, a research and development company in Palo Alto, in December 1979. Here they saw for the first time Xerox's graphical user interface (GUI) and Jobs was adamant that this was the future of computing. Jobs negotiated three days use of Xerox's facilities in exchange for $1,000,000 of pre-IPO stock, and that was all the time they needed to dream up the core features of the Apple Lisa, the first personal computer aimed at individual business users to have a GUI. Xerox undoubtedly did well out of this deal too: the pre-IPO price that they negotiated was just $10.

Lesson No. 14: Compatibility with related products, current and future, is important.

1980 was a bumper year for Apple - Jobs launched the Apple III in May, and the company had received attention-grabbing coverage in both *Kilobaud Microcomputing* (the leading magazine for computer hobbyists) and the *Financial Times* - and so on December 12, Apple launched its initial public offering (IPO). When Apple went public, it immediately created 300 millionaires (more than any other company in history), and it raised more capital than any US firm since the Ford Motor Company in 1956. The market was buzzing, and investors and commentators alike wanted a slice of the Apple pie. The opening price for Apple shares was $22, so Xerox instantly made a fortune, as did many other venture capitalists who had backed the company in its earliest days.

Lesson No. 15: Be generous to all your stakeholders. You can achieve success and wealth together.

Apple's first shareholder meeting as a public company took place in January 1981. Jobs took to the floor with pre-prepared speech, but a short way into the meeting he abandoned his script and spoke from the heart. Investors bought into the Jobs brand, and that of Apple, and his charisma and passion for his products spoke volumes. Jobs exuded confidence and was able to enthuse other people. Just as he had been able to entice Mike Scott to join Apple from National Superconductor in 1978, when Jobs stretched out a hand to John Sculley (then President of Pepsi Cola) to become Apple's CEO in 1983, Sculley wouldn't have dreamed of refusing. Jobs knew that having the right team at Apple was the key to its long-term success, and he wasn't afraid to tell people so:

> *My model for business is The Beatles. They were four guys who kept each other's kind of negative tendencies in check. They balanced each other and the total was greater than the sum of the parts. That's how I see business: great things in business are never done by one person, they're done by a team of people.*

Lesson No. 16: Surround yourself with brilliance.

The product that put Apple on the map, more than any other (at least in the company's formative years) was the Macintosh, the first mass-produced personal computer with an integral GUI and a computer mouse to control it. The Macintosh took its name from the designer Jef Raskin's favourite kind of apple (the McIntosh), but as another company (McIntosh Laboratory Inc) already owned that brand name, and refused to give Jobs a release for the name, the spelling change was necessary.

Jobs was personally emotionally attached to the Macintosh, as were many members of its development team. He told *Playboy* magazine about it in 1985:

> *I don't think I've ever worked so hard on something, but working on Macintosh was the neatest experience of my life. Almost everyone who worked on it will say that. None of us wanted to release it at the end. It was as though we knew that once it was out of our hands, it wouldn't be ours anymore. When we finally presented it at the shareholders' meeting, everyone in the auditorium gave it a five-minute ovation. What was incredible to me was that I could see the Mac team in the first few rows. It was as though none of us could believe we'd actually finished it. Everyone started crying.*

It was also when Jobs was working on the Macintosh that his colleague Bud Tribble first coined the phrase "reality distortion field" (RDF) to describe Jobs' ability to convince himself (and everyone else) that what seemed to be impossible was, in fact, possible. He used a mixture of charisma, bravado, hyperbole and dogged persistence to get his message through, though critics have suggested Jobs did sometimes allow the distortion of reality to run too far. Although that his colleagues were aware of it, they were easily falling into the RDF, this is how inspirational and motivational Steve Jobs was a leader of his team.

Lesson No. 17: Build and sell great products that you believe in.

The public product launch of the Macintosh was second to none, before or since. Apple spent $2.5 million buying all 39 advertising pages in a special edition of *Newsweek*; they inserted an 18-page brochure in numerous other magazines; and they ran their now-infamous *1984* commercial, directed by Ridley Scott, at the Super Bowl. That single national broadcast cost Apple $1.5 million, and the advert parodied scenes from George Orwell's dystopian novel, *Nineteen Eight-Four*. The advert's heroine wore a Macintosh emblazoned on her t-shirt, and together they saved the world from conformity. The response from Apple's shareholders was ecstatic.

Lesson No. 18: Be persistent. Be persuasive.

The Macintosh went on sale two days after the advert aired at the Super Bowl. The company ran a "Test Drive a Macintosh" promotion, a new idea whereby anyone with a credit card could borrow a computer for 24 hours to test it out at home. 200,000 consumers participated in the promotion (far in excess of Apple's predictions), and demand was so high that Apple could not not make machines fast enough to meet it. They increased the price from $1,995 to $2,495, and still consumers flocked to the stores.

The GUI on the Macintosh was completely new, and existing forms of software had to be re-written in order to be compatible with it. In order to avoid being written off as a novelty item, Apple therefore had to develop their own software that worked with their new platform. Apple bundled two programs with the computer when you bought it, MacWrite and Mac-Paint, encouraged Microsoft and Linux to develop Mac-compatible versions, and launched their own Macintosh Office before the end of 1985. These moves were Apple's first ventures into software, but Jobs recognised that his machines would never dominate the market unless there were sufficient, high-quality programs to run on them.

Lesson No. 19:People who are serious about software should make their own hardware.

Although Jobs was charming and persuasive, he was also disorganised and erratic in his management style. Colleagues remember Jobs running meetings into the early hours of the morning and then still expecting staff to be at their desks for seven the following morning. This inevitably caused tensions in the office, particularly with the newly-appointed Sculley. The working relationship between the two men deteriorated substantially. Jobs attempted to oust his CEO but failed. The move backfired terribly: Apple's board of directors gave Sculley the authority to remove Jobs from all posts bar that of Chairman, and then they stripped him of his management duties too. Jobs stopped coming to work and resigned completely five months later.

Lesson No. 20: Stay hungry, stay foolish.

Part 3: The Next Step

Bruised from his ignominious departure from Apple, which had been the dominant feature in his life for the past decade, Jobs toyed briefly with the idea of crossing the Iron Curtain and opening a computer company in the USSR, and he also applied (unsuccessfully) to brome a civilian astronaut onboard the International Space Station. With the commercial responsibility of Apple lifted from his shoulders, Jobs became happier and more creative: in a speech at Stanford University in 2005 he would look back on his firing from Apple as the best thing that could possibly have happened to him. He reflected, "I'm pretty sure none of this would have happened if I hadn't been fired from Apple. It was awful-tasting medicine, but I guess the patient needed it."

Lesson No. 21: Look critically at yourself, know your mistakes, and work hard to fix them. No one else is going to do this for you.

Jobs had sold all bar one of his 6.5 million Apple shares, and had consequently pocketed $70 million, an eye-watering sum at any point in history, but especially in 1985. Using the experience he had gained at Apple, the first thing he did was to invest $7 million of his own money into a new venture, NeXT, and he partnered with billionaire investor Ross Perot.

Jobs used the expertise he had gained from Apple but crucially in this new company, where he alone made the decisions, he could take the products in the direction he wanted to. He had ideas about architecture he wanted to pursue, and he set off and tried them out.

Lesson No. 22: Don't be afraid to be a beginner again. There's a phrase in Buddhism, 'Beginner's mind.' It's wonderful to have a beginner's mind.

Priced at $9,999, the first NeXT computer was too expensive for home and education users it had originally been designed for. It did, however, contain experimental technologies such as digital signal processor chips, a built-in Ethernet port, and a Mach kernal, and these innovative features made it attractive to the financial, scientific, and academic communities.

Jobs identified this interest and galvanised the media to cover the lavish gala event that marked the product's launch. Jobs' hunch that the NeXT was best suited as a research machine was right: whilst he was working at CERN, Tim Berners-Lee invented his browser for the World Wide Web on his NeXT workstation.

Following his gut hunches was important to Jobs, and more often than not they proved correct. He mused on the subject:

You can't connect the dots looking forward; you can only connect them looking backward. So you have to trust that the dots will somehow connect in your future. You have to trust in something — your gut, destiny, life, karma, whatever. This approach has never let me down, and it has made all the difference in my life.

Lesson No. 23: Do what you believe is right, even if it doesn't make sense at the time.

Jobs was not satisfied with the first version of NeXT, however, and so in less than a year he released the NeXTcube. Jobs advertised the NeXTcube as the first 'interpersonal' computer: it was a personal computer that you could use to share voice files, images, graphics, and even video by email. This had never been possible before. Jobs told reporters at the *Computimes* and *New Straits Times* that this marked a revolution in computing, and in many ways this was true. The journalists picked up the message and ran with it.

Lesson No. 24: If you are not satisfied with what you have made, do it again. And this time do it better.

It is in the development of the NeXTcube that we first see Jobs' obsession with aesthetics, a major factor in the success of Apple today. He described his philosophy as follows:

> *When you're a carpenter making a beautiful chest of drawers, you're not going to use a piece of plywood on the back, even though it faces the wall and nobody will see it. You'll know it's there, so you're going to*

*use a beautiful piece of wood on the back.
For you to sleep well at night, the aesthetic,
the quality, has to be carried all the way
through.*

Much to the horror of NeXT's hardware de-
partment, Jobs demanded that the NeXTcube
be given a magnesium case. This was not
only more expensive but more difficult to work
with than earlier plastic cases. Jobs won the
argument by force of personality, however,
and from then on he has always been associ-
ated with developing products that are as vi-
sually appealing as they are functional.

***Lesson No. 25: Functionality and design
go hand in hand when you are developing
a desirable product.***

Jobs understood from his experience with
the Macintosh that users wanted first-rate
software to run on their new machines, and he
encouraged software developers to design
NeXT compatible programs. The machines
came with *Mathematica* (a program for those
working in the scientific, engineering, mathe-
matical and computing fields) pre-installed,
Tim Berners-Lee made the first web browser
for NeXT platforms, and by the early 1990s
there were also a number of computer games
available for NeXT machines, including *Doom,*

Heretic, and *Quake*. It was possible to install the *Meriam-Webster Dictionary* and the *Complete Works of Shakespeare* too, should you feel so inclined.

NeXT computers at first had their own, proprietary operating system, NeXTSTEP, but within a year of the launch of the first NeXT machines, Jobs realised that it was the operating system, rather than the computer hardware, that would make NeXT a fortune. He therefore took the bold step of re-orientating the company's business strategy. He oversaw the development of a PC compatible version of NeXTStep in 1991, held a demo of it at the NeXTWorld Expo in January 1992, and by the middle of 1993, the software was selling well to corporate clients. Industry trend setters such as Chrysler, First Chicago NBC and the Swiss Bank Corporation, as well as government bodies including the Central Intelligence Agency, the National Security Agency, and the Naval Research Laboratory, installed the operating system, and their belief in the software encouraged others to follow suit.

Lesson No. 26: Turn consumers into evangelists, not just customers

Under Jobs' leadership, NeXT stopped making hardware completely in 1993 and concentrated on software alone. Sun Microsystems invested $10 million in NeXT, and together Jobs and Sun's CEO, Scott McNealy, built a new operating system called OpenStep, a version of which was available for Microsoft Windows. More important than this, however, was their launch of WebObjects, a platform for building large-scale dynamic web applications. This software was adopted by the BBC, Disney, WorldCom and Dell, as well as other major international players, and it was this single product that made NeXT such a desirable acquisition target for Apple in 1996 (see *Part 4: Return to Apple*).

Lesson No. 27: Focus on your strengths.

Whilst at NeXT, Jobs experiments with original business management strategies as well as new products. He wanted to create a completely new corporate culture and to improve the sense of community at the company. Jobs emphasised the point that his staff were not employees but rather members of the company, and as such they were entitled to many benefits: until 1990s there were only two basic salary plans on offer, $75,000 to those who joined before 1986, and $50,000 to those who joined after. Performance reviews took place every six months, and if you did well, you would be offered a pay rise. Staff were paid monthly in advance (rather than bi-weekly in arrears, as was the custom in Silicon Valley at the time), and the company health insurance plan was available to unmarried and same-sex couples as well as married couples.

NeXT's offices, designed by architect I M Pei, were almost entirely open plan: only Jobs' office and the conference rooms were enclosed. This fostered a sense of oversight by and of your peers, and so encouraged staff to work harder.

Lesson No. 28: Build the right environment, to inspire creativity and hard work.

Although Jobs dedicated much of his time and effort to NeXT, it was not his only commercial interest at this time. He bought The Graphics Group from Lucasfilm in 1986 for $10 million and renamed the company Pixar. Although Jobs had no creative experience (beyond taking a calligraphy course in college), he did understand the technology behind computer graphics and believed he could take the company into a new phase in digital animation.

Pixar's first film, in 1995, was *Toy Story*, and Jobs was the executive producer. Other box office hits included *A Bug's Life* (1998), *Monsters Inc* (2001), *Finding Nemo* (2003) and *The Incredibles* (2004), and Pixar won the Academy Award for Best Animated Feature seven times. Jobs was fast becoming a force to be reckoned with in the film world as well as in the world of computers.

Lesson No. 29: Don't limit yourself. Spread your creativity into different areas.

All of these films had been distributed through Disney, and in the run-up to the expiry of this distribution contract, Jobs was responsible for renegotiating the deal with Disney's chief executive, Michael Eisner. Despite Jobs' efforts, the renegotiation efforts floundered, but Eisner was replaced by Bob Iger in late 2005, and the story took an unexpected twist. Iger offered to buy Pixar from Jobs and his partners for an all-stock transaction worth $7.4 billion. Jobs jumped at the opportunity and consequently became the largest single shareholder, owning 7% of Disney's shares. He also joined Disney's board of directors.

Lesson No. 30: Make sure you diversify your portfolio. Spreading your risk across multiple businesses can generate unexpected returns.

Part 4: Return to Apple

Throughout the 1990s, under the successive leaderships of Sculley (1983 to '93), Michael Spindler (1993 to '96) and Gil Amelio (1996 to '97), Apple was struggling commercially, so much so that Amelio described the company as being, "like a ship with a hole in the bottom, leaking water." The IBM PC was dominating the computer market and had a comparable GUI; Apple's new product lines (which included Centris, Quadra and Performa) were poorly marketed and sold erratically; and in 1995 the decision was taken to license the Mac OS and Macintosh ROMs to third party manufacturers, short-sightedly removing the Macintosh's unique selling point (USP).

Lesson No. 31: With the wrong person at the helm, even a strong company can take a turn for the worse.

What Apple's directors did do, however, was realise their shortcomings, and in particular that they needed a new generation operating system to take the company forward into the 21st century. NeXT and Be Inc competed against each other in the bid process, and NeXT emerged from the battle triumphant. Apple acquired NeXT for $419 million in cash, and Jobs personally received 1.5 million shares in Apple.

Jobs was invited back to Apple, initially as a consultant in December 1996 (when Amelio was ousted) and then, seven months later, he was appointed as interim CEO, a position which would be made permanent in 2000. Way back in 1985, in an interview with *Playboy* magazine, Jobs had told the reporter:

> *I'll always stay connected with Apple. I hope that throughout my life I'll sort of have the thread of my life and the thread of Apple weave in and out of each other, like a tapestry. There may be a few years when I'm not there, but I'll always come back.*

Unwittingly he had foretold his own future.

Lesson No. 32: Be patient, and be humble.

Jobs' return was a breath of fresh air into a company that had become increasingly stagnant in its ideas, projects and personnel. Jobs terminated research and development projects he didn't feel had long-term viability (including Cyberdog, Newton and OpenDoc); he identified a loop hole in the Mac OS licensing contracts and used it to terminate them;

and he shook up the company's management structure.

Salon magazine reported that after Jobs' return, Apple employees tried to avoid stepping into a lift with him, "afraid that they might not have a job when the doors opened," but in reality only a few members of staff suffered this fate. Jobs did restructure Apple's board of directors, however, parachuting in some of the best executives from NeXT and so allowing the two companies to fully merge.

Lesson No. 33: Don't be afraid to make difficult decisions, the ones who are crazy enough to think they can change the world are usually the ones that do.

Journalists were keen to report on Jobs being the single-handed saviour of Apple, but he didn't see it that way. When asked by BusinessWeek in May 1998 if his return would reinvigorate the company with a sense of magic, Jobs replied:

You're missing it. This is not a one-man show. What's reinvigorating this company is two things: One, there's a lot of really talented people in this company who listened to the world tell them they were losers for a couple of years, and some of them were on

the verge of starting to believe it them-
selves. But they're not losers. What they
didn't have was a good set of coaches, a
good plan. A good senior management
team. But they have that now.

His humility over this issue won him a great
deal of respect amongst his Apple colleagues
and the wider tech community.

Lesson No. 34: Respect your team.

Apple's corporate recovery had begun, and
Jobs was the man with both the vision and his
hand on the rudder. Although he probably had
only an inkling of it at the time, things for
Apple were about to get very exciting indeed.

Using NeXT's WebObjects application as
its basis, Jobs launched the Apple Store in
November 1997. WebObjects meant that the
Apple Store was quick to build - it took less
than a year to design it and make it opera-
tional - and in the first month of trading, the
Apple Store generated $12 million in orders.
This was the first time that Apple had had a
direct sales outlet: until now it had always sold
products through third party agents. The direct
sales model also enabled Jobs to implement
his new manufacturing strategy, one where
products were built to order.

The built to order model (also known as just in time, or JIT) is a concept developed in Japan by Toyota in the 1950s as part of their philosophy of Lean Management, and it was something Jobs had trialled when building the offices for NeXT. When properly implemented, it enables a company to improve its return on investment by reducing its inventory and carrying costs. JIT requires precision and organisation, but at Apple it proved very effective indeed.

The launch of the Apple Store online was the first part of this process: physical Apple Stores would open from 2001 onwards, optimising product visibility in the marketplace and ensuring it was Apple, not an intermediary, who would earn the lion's share of the profits on retail sales.

Lesson No. 35: Control the full user experience from the product itself, even to the buying experience.

Although Apple and Microsoft had a historic rivalry, Jobs took to the stage at the 1997 Macworld Expo to announce a five-year partnership with Microsoft. Microsoft agreed to release Microsoft Office for use on the Macintosh platform and make a token investment of $150 million into Apple; and in exchange,

Apple settled a long-running dispute as to whether or not Microsoft Windows infringed Apple patents, and announced that Internet Explorer (a Microsoft product) would henceforth be the default web browser on Apple's machines.

Jobs was very much the public mouthpiece of Apple, and so people listened when he spoke. In reality, few people were interested in the minutiae of the partnership deal, but they did respond favourably to his over arching message:

> If we want to move forward and see Apple healthy and prospering again, we have to let go of a few things here. We have to let go of this notion that for Apple to win, Microsoft has to lose. We have to embrace a notion that for Apple to win, Apple has to do a really good job. And if others are going to help us that's great, because we need all the help we can get, and if we screw up and we don't do a good job, it's not somebody else's fault, it's our fault. So I think that is a very important perspective. If we want Microsoft Office on the Mac, we better treat the company that puts it out with a little bit of gratitude; we like their software.

So, the era of setting this up as a competition between Apple and Microsoft is over as far as I'm concerned. This is about getting Apple healthy, this is about Apple being able to make incredibly great contributions to the industry and to get healthy and prosper again.

Lesson No. 36: Find an enemy! Great rivalries are the best advertisement.

With the wind in his sales, and the highly regarded reputation of Microsoft as an added boost, Jobs strode confidently into 1998 and the start of an extraordinary period of innovation for Apple. The company would transform the world of consumer electronics with the launch of the iMac, the iBook, the iPod and, of course, Mac OS.

Yet again, Jobs emphasised the importance of aesthetics in the design process for the iMac.

Design is a funny word. Some people think design means how it looks. But of course, if you dig deeper, it's really how it works. The design of the Mac wasn't what it looked like, although that was part of it. Primarily, it was how it worked. To design something really well, you have to get it. You have to really grok what it's all about. It takes a passionate commitment to really thoroughly understand something, chew it up, not just quickly swallow it. Most people don't take the time to do that.

The 'i', imaginatively, stood for Internet, individuality and innovation, and was the brainchild of Ken Segall, an employee at an LA advertising agency. Jobs had originally wanted to call the new machine MacMan, but he recognised the superiority of Segall's suggestion and adopted it.

Lesson No. 37: Call an expert when you need to.

The selling point of the iMac was its simplicity: users wanted out-of-the-box experiences, and this is exactly what Jobs gave them, even when it was hard to deliver.

That's been one of my mantras — focus and simplicity. Simple can be harder than complex: You have to work hard to get your thinking clean to make it simple. But it's worth it in the end because once you get there, you can move mountains.

It wasn't just rhetoric, however. Jobs practised what he preached. In one famous TV commercial, a seven year old and his dog were challenged to set up an iMac, racing against a Stanford University MBA student with an HP Pavilion 8250. The child and the dog were ready to go after eight minutes and

15 seconds; the MBA student was left trailing in the dust.

Lesson No. 38: Keep the design simple, and when you get there, simplify it even more.

Even more revolutionary than the iMac, however, was the iBook, the first consumer orientated laptop computer. The first model, the iBook G3, was nicknamed "the clamshell", and Jobs unveiled it during his keynote speech at the Macworld Conference and Expo in New York in June 1999.

The iBook was available in multiple bright colours (setting it apart from its cream or black competitors), and it was the first mainstream computer designed and sold with integrated wireless networking (wireless LAN). USB, Ethernet and modem ports all came as standard, as did the optical drive. The shape of the machine, which included an integral handle, was attractive and functional in equal measure, and it was also durable and very reliable. Consumers loved it and the iBook sold like hot cakes. It was the first laptop to be bought en-masse for schools.

Lesson No. 39: Don't sell products, sell dreams.

Two significant Apple product launches went hand in hand in 2001: iTunes and the iPod. Napster had already made online music sales a reality, and it was inevitable therefore that Apple would follow them into the market-place.

Selling music was not enough for Jobs, however: he knew that people would not be satisfied sitting at home listening to music on their computers but rather would want to listen to the tracks they had purchased out and about, just as they could do with a Walkman or portable CD player. Early examples of digital music players were available to buy, but as Greg Joswiak, Apple's vice president of iPod product marketing, told *Newsweek*, "The products stank." Jobs knew that Apple could do better.

As with the iMac, the strength of the iPod lay in its combination of aesthetics and function. Jobs pulled together a team of masters in their respective arts, including hardware engineers Jon Rubinstein, Tony Fadell, and Michael Dhuey. They took inspiration wherever they could find it: Rubinstein discovered and purchased the rights to the Toshiba disk drive from Toshiba in Japan; the wheel based user interface was inspired by a Bang &

Olufsen BeoCom 6000 telephone; and the shape came from a 1958 Braun T3 transistor radio. Jobs decided not to use Apple's in-house software but looked for ideas outside: he settled on PortalPlayer's reference platform and an interface developed by Pixo, whose staff he supervised directly.

Jobs had no qualms at all about taking ideas from other companies and using them in new ways. For him, such stealing didn't have negative connotations but was rather part of the creative process. He explained:

Ultimately, it comes down to taste. It comes down to trying to expose yourself to the best things that humans have done and then try to bring those things into what you're doing. Picasso had a saying: good artists copy, great artists steal. And we have always been shameless about stealing great ideas, and I think part of what made the Macintosh great was that the people working on it were musicians and poets and artists and zoologists and historians who also happened to be the best computer scientists in the world.

The first iPod was Mac compatible, had a 5GB hard drive, and could store around 1,000 songs.

Lesson No. 40: You don't have to be the first, but you have to be the best!

Jobs' launch of the iPod is important because it marks the point when Apple branched out from computers to consumer electronics. Jobs was a visionary, and he knew in his heart that the future of electronics and computers was not in desktop machines but in multi-function, portable devices, and in the computer programs to run on them. This shift in focus was made explicit in Apple's name change from Apple Computers Inc. to Apple Inc., which Jobs announced to the public during his keynote address at the January 2007 Macworld Expo.

The miniaturisation of components for the iPod of course led the way for the creation of the iPhone and the iPad. The revolutionary iPhone was, in essence, a widescreen iPod with the world's first mobile video voicemail service, and a fully-functional version of Safari, Apple's web browser. It was released to the public in July 2007 and took the mobile telecommunications market by storm, knocking market leaders Blackberry and Nokia into the dust almost overnight.

The iPad, launched in January 2010, filled the market gap between the iPhone and the iMac, and though commentators initially feared the iPad would take interest away from the iPhone and iMac, no such thing happened: consumers bought into the brand identity and wanted to own all three items. What is more, Jobs' obsession with his products' appearance meant that for the first time, electronics were cool. New iPhone models were released on a 12-month cycle, and committed fans had to have the new version immediately, every time it was released. New software functions such as Photobooth and FaceTime, and hardware features such as both front and rear-facing cameras made every new Apple product irresistible. Apple shot ahead of all its competitors, including long-term rivals Microsoft.

Lesson No. 41: Don't rely on market research, people don't know what they want until you show them.

Jobs was undoubtedly hugely successful and professionally admired by his peers and employees alike, but he wasn't always popular. He was a demanding perfectionist and always wanted to be one step ahead of the game, summarising his view as follows:

We don't get a chance to do that many things, and every one should be really excellent. Because this is our life. Life is brief, and then you die, you know? And we've all chosen to do this with our lives. So it better be damn good. It better be worth it.

The pursuit of perfection, not only for himself but for everyone else, made it incredibly difficult for his colleagues at Apple to keep up with him. In 1993, Jobs made *Fortune* magazine's list of America's Toughest Bosses, and 14 years later, the same magazine (which was, on the whole, supportive of Jobs and his endeavours), described him as, "one of Silicon Valley's leading egomaniacs."

Lesson No. 42: Don't tolerate bozos around you. Build a team of A players only.

Jobs was not afraid to tackle competition, and his detractors, head on. From the late 1980s Jobs had gone head to head with Michael Dell, CEO of Dell, and they publicly traded words. Jobs called Dell's computers "un-innovative beige boxes" and a decade later, when Apple itself was stuck in the quagmire, Dell suggested that the best thing to do to Apple was to "shut it down and give the money back to the shareholders." Dell could not possibly see into the future, however, and Jobs had the last laugh in 2006 when Apple's market capitalisation finally exceeded Dell's. He sent a two line email out to all Apple employees. It said:

Team, it turned out that Michael Dell wasn't perfect at predicting the future. Based on today's stock market close, Apple is worth more than Dell. Stocks go up and down, and things may be different tomorrow, but I thought it was worth a moment of reflection today. Steve.

Part 5: Death and Legacy

In 2011, Apple had net sales of more than $108 billion and net profits of nearly $26 billion. The Apple iPhone was outselling its nearest competitor, the Samsung Galaxy S II, by seven to one, and the company shifted over 32 million units of the iPad in that year alone, contributing more than a quarter of the company's revenue. Behind the scenes, all was not so well: Jobs had been on medical leave since January, and in August 2011 he dropped the bombshell of his resignation as CEO on health grounds. He remained with the company as chairman of the board, but the markets shook with the shock: Apple's share price fell 5% in after-hours trading. For many people, Jobs' face, his unique leadership style and the commercial success of Apple had become inseparable.

The reality was that Jobs had been sick for a long time: he had first been diagnosed with a cancerous tumour in his pancreas back in 2003, and had announced the fact to his staff at Apple by the middle of 2004. Although the prognosis for pancreatic cancer is poor, and Jobs was suffering from a particularly rare form, an islet cell neuroendocrine tumour, Jobs resisted medical intervention for the first nine months, attempting to combat the disease through changes to his diet.

Jobs' reality distortion field, which had proved so effective when creating consumer products, blinded him to the seriousness of his condition, but on this occasion, force of personality and self-belief was not enough to overturn the medical reality.

Harvard researcher Ramzi Amri, writing later in the *Daily Mail*, suggested that this delay in seeking conventional medical treatment reduced Jobs' long-term survival chances to next to none. Jobs later regretted the situation, as he confided to his biographer, Walter Isaacson.

Jobs tried following a vegan diet, acupuncture, herbal remedies, juice fasts, bowel cleansings and even consulted a psychic. None of these alternative approaches worked, and he went under the knife for the first time in July 2004. The pancreaticoduodenectomy, also known as the Whipple procedure, was a major surgical operation and appeared to successfully remove the tumour.

Lesson No. 43: Sometimes you have to follow the traditional methods, especially when it is a matter of life and death.

Jobs was not afraid to speak out about illness and death, though he understandably preferred to discuss it as though it were one step removed from himself. In 2005 he gave an important address at Stanford University, which summed up his views:

No one wants to die. Even people who want to go to heaven don't want to die to get there. And yet death is the destination we all share. No one has ever escaped it. And that is as it should be, because Death is very likely the single best invention of Life. It is Life's change agent. It clears out the old to make way for the new. Right now the new is you, but someday not too long from now, you will gradually become the old and be cleared away. Sorry to be so dramatic, but it is quite true…

Your time is limited, so don't waste it living someone else's life. Don't be trapped by dogma — which is living with the results of other people's thinking. Don't let the noise of others' opinions drown out your own inner voice. And most important, have the courage to follow your heart and intuition. They somehow already know what you truly want to become. Everything else is secondary.

Lesson No. 44: Live your life to the full, personally and professionally, because no one ever knows how long they have on earth.

The honeymoon period from cancer was brief: journalists watching Jobs' keynote speech at Apple's 2006 Worldwide Developers Conference described his as looking thin, gaunt and listless, in stark contrast to his usual lively deliveries. The official Apple line was that Jobs was in good health, but rumours abounded, and shareholders started asking questions, saying that they had a right to know. *Bloomberg* inadvertently published a 2,500 word obituary of Jobs in August 2008, to which Jobs responded, tongue in cheek, "Reports of my death are greatly exaggerated." It was a line he'd taken from Mark Twain.

Jobs and his Apple colleagues tried to avoid answering questions about his health, declaring that it was a private matter for Jobs and his family, but at the start of 2009 when Jobs was too unwell to deliver the final keynote address at the Macworld Conference and Expo, he had to come clean. He initially put his problems down to a hormone imbalance, but then announced he had "learned that my health-related issues are more complex than I originally thought". Jobs announced a six-month leave of absence, appointing Tim Cook as acting CEO, and underwent a liver transplant in Memphis in April of that year. CNN reported that his prognosis was "excellent".

Lesson No. 45: When you are the face of an international company, your private business becomes everybody's business.

After his transplant, Jobs returned to Apple and worked for 18 months. He oversaw the launch of a wealth of innovative new products, from Mac OS X Snow Leopard and the Magic Trackpad, to iPads with Wi-Fi and 3G and new models of the MacBook, iPhone and Mac Mini. The buzz around new Apple products, though stimulating, was also exhausting, and again in January 2011 Jobs announced his leave of absence on medical grounds. He continued to make public appearances, including at the public launches of the iPad 2 and iCloud, but the cancer had returned aggressively and was taking its toll.

Jobs stepped down as Apple's CEO on 24 August, 2011, telling the board of directors, "I have always said if there ever came a day when I could no longer meet my duties and expectations as Apple's CEO, I would be the first to let you know. Unfortunately, that day has come." He appointed Tim Cook as his successor as CEO but continued as chairman of the board.

Lesson No. 46: Know when it is the right time to step down and let someone else take the reins.

Six weeks after Jobs stepped down, he lost consciousness and died the following day, surrounded by his wife, children and sisters. He had suffered from complications relating to a relapse in his pancreatic cancer. Apple, Microsoft and Disney all flew their flags at half mast as a mark of respect. For the next two weeks Apple's corporate home page carried a portrait of Jobs, his name and his dates of birth and death, as well as the following obituary:

> *Apple has lost a visionary and creative genius, and the world has lost an amazing human being. Those of us who have been fortunate enough to know and work with Steve have lost a dear friend and an inspiring mentor. Steve leaves behind a company that only he could have built, and his spirit will forever be the foundation of Apple.*

Jobs was buried in his hometown of Palo Alto in a non-denominational cemetery. His grave is unmarked and his funeral was a private affairs for family and close friends. Separate memorial services were held for invited guests (including Bono, Yo Yo Ma and Jobs' former girlfriend, Joan Baez) at Stanford University, and also a few days later on the Apple Campus for Apple staff. Many of Apple's stores closed for the day so that employees could attend the service.

Lesson No. 47: Even Superman has to die sometime.

Jobs' death was front page news around the world. More than a million people left tributes. *Time* magazine and Bloomberg's *Businessweek* both published commemorative issues with Jobs on the cover. US President Barack Obama, UK Prime Minister David Cameron and Microsoft founder Bill Gates all spoke out about Jobs' contribution to society. Jobs was characterised as the Henry Ford or Thomas Edison of his time. In life, Jobs did have his detractors, but after his death these people were largely silent.

In the years running up to his death, Jobs had collected every award and accolade imaginable: he was induced into the California

Hall of Fame by California Governor Arnold Schwarzenegger in 2007; *Fortune* magazine named him the most powerful person in business in 2007 and CEO of the decade in 2009; in 2010 *Forbes* magazine ranked him at No. 17 on their list, The World's Most Powerful People; and he was the *Financial Times'* person of the year 2010.

The tributes didn't stop with Jobs' death, however. When in 2012 young adults were asked to name the greatest innovator of all time, Jobs ranked second, only behind Thomas Edison. He was posthumously awarded the Grammy Trustees Award for his services to the music industry, and a write-up in Forbes magazine described him as both the "greatest entrepreneur of our time" and "the quintessential entrepreneur of our generation".

Lesson No. 48: Be an inspiration for the next generation.

What, though, was Jobs' legacy to the world? Firstly, Jobs made technology cool in a way it had never been before. He was not only the face of Apple, but of Silicon Valley and the computer industry as a whole. The prevailing view prior to Jobs' return to Apple, in the words of Sculley, was that "High-tech could not be designed and sold as a consumer product." Jobs knew that innovation demanded people who could dream up the things others believed were impossible, and were crazy enough to act on their ideas. One of his speeches on the topic was particularly telling:

> *Here's to the crazy ones, the misfits, the rebels, the troublemakers, the round pegs in the square holes... The ones who see things differently — they're not fond of rules... You can quote them, disagree with them, glorify or vilify them, but the only thing you can't do is ignore them because they change things... They push the human race forward, and while some may see them as the crazy ones, we see genius, because the ones who are crazy enough to think that they can change the world, are the ones who do.*

Jobs' vision of turning Apple into a consumer products company was said to be a lunatic plan, and he was completely happy about that: it confirmed that he was one of the crazy people, the rebels he admired. His plan worked because Jobs understood better than either his colleagues or his competitors what the future marketplace would look like and what the demands of consumers would be. Jobs was the man who took the tech industry out of the hands of computer geeks and catapulted it into the mainstream.

Lesson No. 49: Put a dent in the universe.

Unlike Gates at Microsoft, Jobs was not widely known for his philanthropy: he refused to sign Warren Buffet's Giving Pledge and when he returned to Apple in 1997, one of the first things he did was to terminate the company's corporate philanthropy programmes. In actual fact, it was not that Jobs wasn't generous and didn't believe in charity: like so many other things in his life, he just preferred to do it his way. It was also that unlike many other billionaires, Jobs didn't want to shout about his good works, preferring that the media concentrate their attention on Apple.

One major initiative Jobs did support through Apple was the Project Red programme, which encourages companies to create red versions of their devices and give the profits to charity. Apple has been the single largest contributor to the Project Red Global Fund since its inception, and the money goes towards fighting AIDS, malaria and tuberculosis. Project Red's chief, Bono, quotes Bono as saying that there is "nothing better than the chance to save lives".

Since his death, Jobs' personal wealth, which was estimated at around $11 billion, has been held in the Steven P. Jobs Trust, run by his widow, Laurene Powell Jobs. The transfer of wealth has made Powell the ninth richest woman in the world. She does not discuss how she spends the money, but she is known to have committed time and funding to the Emerson Collective, which makes grants and investments into education initiatives; College Track, which Powell founded in 1997 to put students from low-income families through college; the East Congo Initiative in Africa, which she has visited with Ben Affleck; and the Dream Act, a piece of proposed legislation which would provide legal status for immigrants who arrived in the US as young children. Laura Arrillaga-Andreessen, a philanthropist, lecturer on philanthropy at Stanford University and a close friend of Powell, estimates that "If you total up in your mind all of the philanthropic investments that Laurene has made that the public knows about, that is probably a fraction of 1 percent of what she actually does."

In 1993, Jobs gave an interview to the Wall Street Journal in which he said, "Being the richest man in the cemetery doesn't matter to me … Going to bed at night saying we've done something wonderful… that's what matters to me." It seems Steve Jobs got his wish after all.

Lesson No. 50: What is important is not that we die, but the legacy we have left behind.

Steve Jobs
1955-2011

Final Thoughts

Steve Jobs changed the world more than any other person in his generation. He was content to be an outsider and a rebel because it gave him the freedom to dream and to try the things that other, more conventional individuals thought to be impossible. His meteoric rise from college drop out to revered multi billionaire and tech sector revolutionary took 30 years and was far from a smooth ride, but he had complete and unshakeable faith in his own abilities and was adamant that innovative thinking and hard work would pay inestimable dividends in the long-term. Jobs was right.

In this book we have learned 50 unique lessons from Jobs, his life and work. Although they do stand independently, and it is right to think about each of them in turn, there are also five important, over-arching lessons that encompass many of the smaller points.

1. Work with the best people in the business

If you want to develop the best products in the world, you need the best people in every post. However great you are, you need to delegate responsibility to others, and should ensure that appointments and promotions are given on the basis of expertise (even if it has been gained in other industries) rather than just because someone has worked with you for a long time. Trust the people you appoint, even if they are critical of you, and invest time, money and effort in your commercial relationships so that your staff are loyal and passionate ambassadors for you and your brand.

2. Always be a step ahead of the competition

In business, there is no point looking backwards: you need to look into the future and anticipate customer needs and wants. Keeping ahead requires you to have a never-ending stream of new ideas. They won't always work out, but you will always have something fresh on the drawing board. Don't let your imagination be limited by present realities: research and development can take many years, and by the time you are ready to launch (especially if you are in the driving seat of innovation), technology will more likely than not have caught up and be able to meet your requirements.

3. Believe passionately in what you do.

Passion and commitment sell products. If you don't believe 110% in what you are doing, find something else to do. To be a success, you will have to commit all your time, energy and money to your projects. We all only get one life, so if the project doesn't thrill you to the core, don't waste your life pursuing it. Stop, look around for another idea, and chase after that one instead.

4. Getting something wrong doesn't mean you have failed.

Everyone makes mistakes. It is how we deal with those set-backs that sets successful people apart from those who fail. Jobs launched some dud products. He got kicked out of his own company. He didn't let it get him down. He got back up and fought on but, and this is very important, he did so without resentment. He looked critically at himself and what he had done wrong, and he learned important lessons for the future. When Jobs returned to Apple in 1997, he wasn't the same CEO he had been when he resigned from the company years before. We all have to change, and we all have room to improve.

5. Be the change you want to see in the world.

Saying that you want to change the world is not enough. Your actions need to support your rhetoric. Jobs knew that to revolutionise the tech sector he needed not only to design and release revolutionary products, but to set the bar higher for the entire industry. He then branched out beyond computing, encouraging others sectors to prioritise innovation and quality too. The ethos he created and espoused, of always striving to be and do the best best, and then breaking your own records, will continue at Apple and in Silicon Valley as a whole long after Jobs' death.

Jobs would say that you shouldn't just aim to be an entrepreneur or an inventor. You must be a revolutionary too.

Thank you for purchasing my book! I know you could have picked from dozens of books about Steve Jobs, but you took a chance with mine and I appreciate it.

Made in the USA
Middletown, DE
20 December 2016